DENMARK TRAVEL GUIDE BOOK 2023

Uncovering the Hidden Gems of Denmark

Kian Wright

Disclaimer

The information contained in this book is for general information purposes only.

The information is provided by the author and while we endeavour to keep the information up to date and correct, we make no representations or warranties of any kind, express or implied, about the completeness, accuracy, reliability, suitability, or availability concerning the book or the information, products, services, or related graphics contained in the book for any purpose. Any reliance you place on such information is therefore strictly at your own risk. In no event will the author or publisher be liable for any loss or damage including without limitation, indirect or consequential loss or damage, or any loss or damage

3

whatsoever arising from loss of data or profits arising out of, or in connection with, the use of this Book.

Please note that this disclaimer is subject to change without notice.

TABLE OF CONTENT

INTRODUCTION

Getting to Know Denmark: A Brief Overview

Planning Your Trip to Denmark: A Step-by-Step Guide

Exploring Copenhagen: The Capital
City of Denmark

Best places to eat, drink, shop, and stay
in Denmark

Possible itinerary for a 7-day and 10
days trips to Denmark

Touring North Jutland: Home to
Beautiful Scenery and Beaches

Experiencing Denmark's Culture: Food,
Music, and Art

Understanding the Danish Way of Life:
Customs and Traditions

Understanding the Danish Way of Life:
Customs and Traditions

Outdoor Activities in Denmark That you can participate on: Hiking, Biking, and More

Outdoor Activities in Denmark That you can participate on: Hiking, Biking, and More

Exploring Danish History: Castles, Museums, and Landmarks

Exploring Danish History: Castles, Museums, and Landmarks

Accommodations in Denmark: Hotels, Hostels, and Vacation Rentals

Transportation in Denmark: Getting Around with Ease

Practical Information for Travelers
going to Denmark: Currency, Language,
and Safety

Making the Most of Your Trip: Tips and
Tricks for a Memorable Experience

INTRODUCTION

Welcome to Denmark, a small but mighty country in Northern Europe! Whether you're a first-time visitor or a returning traveller, this comprehensive travel guide will help you discover the best of what Denmark has to offer in 2023.

Denmark is a country of contrasts, with a rich history, beautiful landscapes, charming cities, and a thriving cultural scene. From the bustling streets of

Copenhagen to the peaceful countryside of Jutland, Denmark has something for everyone.

This travel guide is designed to help you plan and make the most of your trip to Denmark.

It includes detailed information on the country's major cities and attractions, as well as practical advice on transportation, accommodations, and safety. You'll also learn about Danish customs and traditions, and get a taste of the country's delicious cuisine and vibrant music and art scene.

Getting to Know Denmark: A Brief Overview

Denmark, a Nordic nation in Northern Europe, is renowned for its high level of living, contemporary way of life, and extensive cultural history. An overview of Denmark is given in this chapter, including information on its geography, history, politics, economics, society, culture, and tourism.

Geography:

With the Jutland Peninsula and more than 400 islands, including Zealand, Funen, and Bornholm, Denmark is a tiny nation in Northern Europe. The Baltic Sea and the North Sea surround the nation, which has a southern border with Germany. Denmark has moderate summers and pleasant winters due to its marine environment.

History:

From the Viking Period, which lasted from the eighth through the eleventh century, Denmark has a lengthy and intricate history. Denmark was a strong monarchy that dominated most of the Baltic Sea area throughout the Middle Ages.

Denmark transitioned to a constitutional monarchy with a democratic form of governance in the 19th century. Although Nazi Germany occupied Denmark during World War Two, the majority of its Jewish community was kept alive. Denmark enlisted in NATO and the EU after the conflict.

Economy:

With a robust welfare state and a high level of economic freedom, Denmark has a mixed-market economy. The nation's service sector is well-developed, and its leading sectors include shipping, alternative energy, medicines, and food manufacturing. Denmark has a high GDP per person and low rates of Hu and income inequality.

Society:

Denmark is a fairly egalitarian country that prides itself on its strong sense of community and a high degree of trust. The nation has a long history of social democracy that emphasizes solidarity, equality, and individual freedom.

The bulk of the people in Denmark are of Danish ancestry, and there are just a few immigrants and refugees. High levels of social welfare, gender equality, and environmental sustainability are hallmarks of the nation.

Culture:

With influences from the Vikings, the Middle Ages, and contemporary Scandinavian design, Denmark has a rich cultural legacy. Danish culture is distinguished by an emphasis on utility, simplicity, and quality of life.

The nation is renowned for its architecture and design, particularly for the creations of Arne Jacobsen and Jorn Utzon. There are several well-known musicians in Denmark, including M, Lukas Graham, and Agnes Obel. Literature, drama, and cinema have a long legacy in the nation.

Tourism:

Denmark is a well-liked travel destination because of its beautiful countryside, cutting-edge cities, and historical sites. The museums, eateries, and nightlife in Copenhagen, the country's capital, make it a sought-after travel destination.

The Legoland theme park in Billund, the Tivoli Gardens amusement park, and the Viking Ship Museum in Roskilde is a few more well-liked tourist destinations. Denmark is renowned for its cycling culture, and there are many beautiful bike paths all around the nation.

Language:

Danish, a North Germanic language spoken by the majority of the people, is the official language of Denmark. In addition to being widely spoken, English is also taught in schools as a second language.

Religion:

The Church of Denmark is the recognized state church of Denmark, where the majority of the population is Lutheran. Yet, Denmark is renowned for its secular and liberal principles, and religion has a very small influence on Danish culture.

Holidays and Festivals:

There are several public holidays celebrated in Denmark, including New Year's Day, Easter, Christmas, and Constitution Day (June 5th).

Midsummer's Eve, when Danes burn bonfires to commemorate the longest day of the year, and Christmas when the streets are decked up with lights and decorations, are two other well-liked occasions for festivities.

Food and beverage:

Danish food is renowned for its simplicity and focus on locally sourced, in-season ingredients. Smrrebrd (open-faced sandwiches), frikadeller (meatballs), and flaeskesteg are popular foods (roast pork). Danish dairy goods, notably butter, and cheese, are extremely well-known worldwide. With several microbreweries and brewpubs spread out around the nation, the craft beer industry is growing there.

Sports:

Denmark has a long history of participation in sports, especially cycling, handball, and football (soccer). In international games, the national football squad has made several noteworthy appearances, notably

winning the 1992 European
Championship.

Several significant international athletic
events, like the 2020 European Football
Championship, have also taken place in
Denmark.

Education:

From the age of six to sixteen, Danish
education is both free and required.
With a well-established system of
elementary, intermediate, and higher
education, the nation places a major
emphasis on high-quality education.
Universities like the University of
Copenhagen and the University of
Aarhus are among those with a strong
worldwide reputation in Denmark.

Conclusion:

Denmark is a fascinating nation with a long history, a contemporary way of life, and a vibrant culture. The nation has become a role model for other countries due to its social welfare system, commitment to environmental sustainability, and emphasis on simplicity and quality of life.

Denmark has plenty to offer everyone, whether they are interested in history, culture, or just experiencing a different way of life.

Denmark is a tiny, wealthy nation with a long history, a solid democracy, and a good standard of living. The welfare state, social cohesiveness, and environmental sustainability of the nation are well-known.

Denmark's culture is distinguished by its emphasis on simplicity, usefulness, and premium design. Denmark is a well-liked travel destination with a combination of ancient sites, contemporary cities, and beautiful countryside.

Planning Your Trip to Denmark: A Step-by-Step Guide

The Scandinavian nation of Denmark is renowned for its beautiful scenery, extensive history, and rich cultural legacy. It is a land of enchanted castles, vibrant structures, delectable cuisine, and hospitable residents. Denmark has lots to offer whether you want a city getaway or a rural escape. We'll provide you with a step-by-step strategy for organizing your vacation to Denmark in this chapter.

NOTE: THIS ASPECT INCLUDES THE LIST OF THINGS YOU SHOULD PREPARE AND HAVE IN MIND AS IT'S NOT A FULL GUIDE OF WHAT YOU NEED TO KNOW ABOUT DENMARK. EVERYTHING NEEDED WILL BE DISCUSSED IN THE OTHER ASPECT OF THIS GUIDE

Step 1:

Choose the Dates of Your Trip

Choosing your travel dates is the first step in organizing your trip to Denmark. The months of May through September are the warmest and longest for travel to Denmark. If you want to go during this time, be sure to reserve your lodging much in advance since it tends to become busy then.

Step 2:

Determine Your Route
From the metropolitan capital of Copenhagen to the charming villages of Roskilde and Odense, Denmark has a lot to offer. You may design your schedule based on your interests and the length of your stay. Among the must-see locations in Denmark are:

Copenhagen: The Little Mermaid Monument, the Tivoli Gardens, and the vibrant Nyhavn Harbor may all be found in Denmark's capital city.

The second-largest city in Denmark is Aarhus, which is renowned for its thriving cultural scene, museums, and parks.

Roskilde: The church, Viking Ship Museum, and music festival are all well-known attractions in this medieval town.

Hans Christian Andersen was born in Odense, a quaint town with cobblestone lanes, half-timbered homes, and a museum honouring the fairy tale creator.

Step 3:

Make hotel reservations

From five-star hotels to affordable hostels, Denmark has a variety of lodging choices. Take into account the location, facilities, and cost while making your hotel reservation. Booking.com, Airbnb, and Hotels.com are a few of the frequently used online travel agencies in Denmark.

Step 4:

Set up the transportation
Denmark has a well-established transportation system that makes getting about the nation simple. Depending on where you're going, you may go by rail, bus, or boat.

Consider buying a Eurail pass, which enables you to travel by train throughout several European nations if you want to visit several places. If you would rather drive, you may also hire a vehicle.

Step 5:

Pack appropriately.
It's important to prepare appropriately since the weather in Denmark may change quickly. Pack layers that you can quickly add or remove depending on the climate, as well as suitable walking shoes and a waterproof raincoat. If you want to go to a rural area, carry insect repellant.

Step 6:

Learn a little Danish

Although the majority of Danes are English speakers, learning a few simple Danish words will greatly enhance your stay. "Tak" (thank you), "hej" (hello), and "marvel" are a few helpful expressions (goodbye).

Step 7:

Investigate regional customs and manners

Danish culture has its traditions and manners, which may vary from your own. For instance, it's nice to come early to a social function and to remove your shoes before entering someone's house. You may prevent cultural misunderstandings and show respect for the local culture by doing some advanced research on these practices and etiquette.

Step 8:

Learn about Danish food
Danish food is a fusion of traditional recipes with cutting-edge, contemporary cooking. Smörrebrd (open-faced sandwiches), frikadeller (meatballs), and fireballer are a few meals you must try (chocolate-covered marshmallows). Don't forget to sample some Danish delicacies like kanelsnegle and wienerbrd (croissants) (cinnamon rolls).

Step 9:

Think of a guided tour

Consider scheduling a guided tour if you want to learn more about Denmark's history and culture. In Denmark, several tour companies provide guided tours of towns, museums, and historical sites. To learn more about the nation's culinary culture and picturesque scenery, you may also schedule food trips and bike tours.

Step 10:

Get travel protection

While it is generally safe to go to Denmark, unforeseen circumstances may still happen. You may have peace of mind in the event of any crises, such as misplaced baggage or a medical emergency, by purchasing travel insurance. Be careful to investigate and contrast several travel insurance plans to locate the one that best meets your requirements.

You may improve your vacation to Denmark and maximize your experience by taking these extra measures. Enjoy yourself, remain safe, and take advantage of all Denmark has to offer.

Conclusion:
It may be thrilling and gratifying to plan a vacation to Denmark. This detailed instruction manual will help you arrange a successful and pleasant vacation. To improve your trip, remember to reserve your lodging well in advance, plan for inclement weather, and learn a few simple Danish words.

Exploring Copenhagen: The Capital City of Denmark

On the eastern side of the island of Zealand stands Copenhagen, the capital of Denmark. With a population of around 1.3 million in the larger metropolitan area, it is the biggest city in Denmark. The city has a long history that dates back to the tenth century, and it has served as Denmark's capital since the fifteenth.

The Little Mermaid monument, which is situated in the harbour and was inspired by the Hans Christian Andersen story, is one of Copenhagen's most recognizable sights. Tivoli Gardens, a historic amusement park, and gardens that date back to 1843, is another well-liked tourist destination.

Copenhagen is renowned for its great culinary scene, which includes many Michelin-starred eateries and a bustling street food market in the hip Nrrebro district. The city is also well-known for its craft beer culture, where several regional brewers create distinctive and mouthwatering brews.

The National Museum of Denmark, the Louisiana Museum of Modern Art, and the Statens Museum für Kunst are just a few of the museums and art galleries located in the city.

The renowned Opera House and the Royal Library are only two examples of the numerous ancient and contemporary buildings in Copenhagen that are well-known for their design and architecture.

Copenhagen boasts a vast network of bike lanes and pathways, making cycling one of the greatest ways to see the city. Moreover, tourists may wander around the vibrant Nyhavn port district or take a canal trip to explore the city from the sea.

Copenhagen is a bustling, interesting city that has something to offer everyone, in general. Visitors visiting Copenhagen are likely to enjoy a great experience because of the city's superb food and drink scene as well as its rich history and culture.

Copenhagen is a city with a special blend of contemporary elegance and old-world charm. The city's stunning architecture, cobblestone streets, and historical sites are clear signs of its long past. Copenhagen is a very traditional city, but it's also highly contemporary, with a big emphasis on sustainability and innovation.

Visits to Copenhagen's many historic sites and attractions are among the greatest ways to explore the city. For instance, the Little Mermaid statue, a recognizable landmark of the city, draws millions of tourists each year.

It is based on the Hans Christian Andersen fable and is situated on a rock in the harbour. The monument may be seen up close by taking a walk around the waterfront or from the sea by taking a boat excursion.

Another well-liked tourist destination in Copenhagen is Tivoli Gardens.

Tivoli Gardens

A historical amusement park and gardens, it was founded in 1843. In addition to thrilling attractions like roller coasters and a Ferris wheel, the park has lovely gardens and a lake. The park comes alive at night with music, shows, and a stunning light display.

Copenhagen is renowned for its culinary and beverage scene. The city is home to a huge selection of eateries, cafés, and pubs that serve both traditional Danish food and fare from across the world.

Visitors may enjoy some of the city's well-known craft beers at one of the numerous local breweries or eat shorebird, a typical Danish open-faced sandwich.

There are several museums and art galleries in Copenhagen for culture and art enthusiasts to explore.

A must-see attraction is the National Museum of Denmark, which has displays of the history, culture, and archaeology of Denmark. Another well-liked destination with an amazing collection of modern and contemporary art is the Louisiana Museum of Modern Art. With its extensive collection of Danish and European art, the Statens Museum för Art is also well worth a visit.

Copenhagen is a fantastic city to explore by bike in addition to its attractions and monuments. The city features a vast network of bike lanes and trails, making cycling around simple and secure. Renting a bike allows visitors to explore the city at their leisure while taking in Copenhagen's sights and noises.

Copenhagen is a city that is full of joys and surprises overall. It is a location that is guaranteed to appeal to tourists of all ages and interests because of its rich history, contemporary attitude, and superb food and drink scene.

Copenhagen offers a variety of activities and sights that may help visitors make lifelong memories. These are some of the best things to do in Copenhagen for tourists:

Visit the statue of the Little Mermaid:

One of Copenhagen's most recognizable monuments and a must-see for travellers is this renowned statue. The monument, which is based on the Hans Christian Andersen story and is situated in the port, is a representation of the city.

Tivoli Gardens exploration:

The gardens and old amusement park in Copenhagen were built in 1843 and are a well-liked tourist destination. This lovely park offers a range of attractions for visitors to enjoy, including rides, gardens, and gardens.

Attempt Danish food:

With several Michelin-starred restaurants and a vibrant street food market, Copenhagen is renowned for its great culinary scene. Visitors may enjoy some of the city's renowned craft brews as well as typical Danish fares like shorebirds and pastries.

Explore the galleries and museums:

The National Museum of Denmark, the Louisiana Museum of Modern Art, and the Statens Museum für Kunst are just a few of the museums and art galleries that can be found in Copenhagen. With these institutions, visitors may learn about the city's rich history and culture.

Visit the canals:

By taking a canal tour, visitors may view the city from the water. These excursions provide guests with a distinctive view of the city and give them a new perspective on some of the well-known attractions.

Do a bicycle tour:

Copenhagen has a vast network of bike lanes and trails, making it the ideal city to tour by bicycle. Renting a bike allows visitors to explore the city at their leisure while taking in Copenhagen's sights and noises.

Get to Nyhavn:

Both visitors and residents like visiting this vibrant port area. One may have a meal or a drink at one of the several restaurants and cafés while taking in the brilliant colours of the buildings as one stroll down the canal.

Take part in the nightlife:

There are several pubs, clubs, and music venues in Copenhagen, which boasts a thriving nightlife scene. By checking out some of the city's well-known venues or going to a concert or performance, tourists may enjoy the vibrant nightlife of the city.

Take a trip to Christiansborg Palace:

The Supreme Court, the Ministry of State, and the Danish Parliament are all housed in this lovely castle. The palace's many chambers and halls, including the throne room and the royal stables, are open to visitors.

Perambulate the botanical garden:

This lovely garden, which lies in the centre of Copenhagen, is home to a sizable collection of international plants and flowers. The various trails in the garden allow visitors to meander across it and take in its breathtaking splendour.

Go to Kronborg Castle for the day:

Shakespeare's Hamlet was supposedly set at this stunning castle, which lies nearby Copenhagen. The many chambers and halls of the castle are open to visitors who want to learn more about its extensive history.

See the Amalienborg Palace Change of the Guard:

The Danish royal family resides at this lovely palace, where guests are welcome to see the daily midday ceremonial of the changing of the guard.

Take a foodie tour:

Visitors may learn more about Copenhagen's vibrant culinary culture by taking a food tour. These trips provide an opportunity to experience traditional Danish cuisine and discover the history of the city's cuisine.

Go to Malmö for the day:

This Swedish city is a terrific destination to spend a day exploring and is just a short train journey from Copenhagen. Tourists may take strolls around the city's many parks and gardens, visit its numerous museums, and take in the breathtaking surroundings.

Discover the street art in the city:

Copenhagen is renowned for having a thriving street art movement, and its walls and structures are covered with many murals and graffiti. Tourists may stroll around the city's many districts and take in numerous pieces of street art.

Here are but a few more suggestions for activities visitors might do to make unforgettable experiences in Copenhagen. Copenhagen is a place that is likely to provide tourists with an outstanding experience thanks to its various attractions, stunning landscape, and vibrant cultural scene.

Best places to eat, drink, shop, and stay in Denmark

Denmark is known for its beautiful landscapes, rich cultural heritage, and culinary delights. This book chapter will provide a guide to the best places to eat, drink, shop, and stay in Denmark.

Best Places to Eat

Copenhagen's Noma

Noma Entrance

Copenhagen's Christianshavn district is home to the two-Michelin-starred restaurant Noma. The restaurant is renowned for its creative Nordic cuisine, which uses regional and seasonal ingredients to create meals that are distinct and delectable.

The eatery is regarded as one of the top restaurants in the world and has been crowned the "World's Best Restaurant" four times by Restaurant Magazine.

Noma places a strong emphasis on sustainability and collaborates closely with regional farmers and producers to guarantee the highest-quality ingredients. The menu offers items like scallops with kelp and dill and reindeer moss, and it often varies.

Copenhagen: Geranium

The three-Michelin-starred restaurant Geranium is situated in Copenhagen's Stepbro district. With an emphasis on sustainable food, the restaurant provides a distinctive dining experience. The menu often varies and includes items like langoustine and ramson as well as sea buckthorn and beets.

A wide variety of natural and organic wines are available, and the restaurant has an exceptional wine list. The dining area is furnished with modern Danish art and has a beautiful view of the surrounding Faelledparken Park.

Danish company Aamanns

Aamanns is a well-liked lunch place in Copenhagen's Stepbro district. Open sandwiches, also known as a shorebird, a classic Danish dish, are the establishment's speciality.

The sandwiches are artfully arranged and produced using seasonal, fresh ingredients.

Other Danish dishes that are available at Aamanns include herring, frikadeller, and pickled vegetables. With a combination of wooden and concrete materials, the restaurant creates a warm and contemporary ambience.

Copenhagen's Fiskebaren

In Copenhagen's hip Meatpacking District sits the seafood restaurant Fiskebaren. The restaurant specialises in Scandinavian cuisine and serves meals made with fresh, sustainable fish. The menu offers items like lobster, mussels, and oysters and is often updated. With an industrial and rustic design and a wide variety of natural and organic wines, the restaurant has a distinctive ambience.

Copenhagen's Sllerd Kro

In the Copenhagen outskirts, there is a historic restaurant called Sllerd Kro. With an emphasis on seasonal and local products, the restaurant offers a combination of classic and contemporary cuisine.

The menu contains items like turbot with green asparagus and morels and roasted pigeon with black garlic and elderflower. The restaurant is located in a stunning structure from the 17th century and boasts a warm, sophisticated environment with a blend of antique and contemporary furnishings.

Copenhagen Alchemist

Located in Copenhagen's Refshaleen district, Alchemy is a three-Michelin-star restaurant. With a 50-course tasting menu that mixes science, art, and cuisine, the restaurant delivers a distinctive and cutting-edge eating experience.

The menu often varies and includes items like truffle with fermented garlic and liquorice and langoustine with caramelised cream and raspberry. The restaurant is situated on a beautiful waterfront and has an industrial, futuristic theme.

Aarhus restaurant Frederikshj

South of Aarhus in the Marselisborg Woods lies the two-Michelin-starred Restaurant Frederikshj. With an emphasis on regional and seasonal ingredients, the restaurant delivers a distinctive fusion of Nordic and French cuisine.

The menu comprises meals like deer with black trumpet mushrooms and beetroot, as well as turbot with oyster and parsley, and it often varies. A combination of ancient and contemporary features creates a warm and beautiful environment in the restaurant.

Copenhagen to Kadeau

In Copenhagen's Christianshavn district sits the one-Michelin-starred eatery Kadeau. With an emphasis on foraged and local products, the restaurant provides a distinctive eating experience.

The menu is always changing and includes delicacies like lamb with chanterelles and pickled berries and razor clams with elderflower and green strawberries.

With a combination of wooden and concrete materials, the restaurant creates a pleasant and rustic ambience.

Copenhagen studio

In Copenhagen's Stepbro district, Studio is a restaurant with one Michelin star. The eatery provides a cutting-edge, contemporary dining experience with an emphasis on sustainable food.

The menu is always changing and includes delicacies like sorrel with white chocolate and yuzu and fowl with chanterelles and rhubarb. The eatery features a view of the neighbourhood lakes, an open kitchen, and a bright, simple design.

Copenhagen, Barr

A Michelin Bib Gourmand establishment called Barr is situated in Copenhagen's Christianshavn district. The eatery provides a relaxed and welcoming eating experience with an emphasis on German and Scandinavian cuisine.

The menu contains delicacies like fish with cucumber and ramson as well as pig belly with cabbage and smoked apple, and it often varies. With a combination of wooden and leather materials, the restaurant offers a warm and rustic aesthetic.

Best Places to Drink

Copenhagen Mikkeller

Copenhagen's Vesterbro district is home to the brewery and taproom Mikkeller. Mikkel Borg Bjergs established the brewery in 2006, and it has since grown to become a well-known craft beer brand worldwide.

In addition to seasonal and experimental brews, the taproom serves a selection of Mikkeller's hallmark beers. With a combination of concrete and wood materials, the room has an industrial and futuristic feel.

Copenhagen, Ruby

A cocktail bar called Ruby may be found in Copenhagen's city centre. With a blend of ancient and contemporary design, the bar creates a refined and elegant ambience.

There are both traditional and contemporary beverages on the cocktail menu, including martinis, negronis, and barrel-aged cocktails. Small meals and bar snacks are also available at Ruby.

Copenhagen, Lidkoeb

The cocktail bar Lidkoeb is situated in Copenhagen's Vesterbro district. The pub, which is located in a historic structure, has a warm, rustic ambience with a combination of wooden and leather furnishings.

Together with a variety of Danish spirits and beers, the cocktail menu offers both traditional and contemporary beverages. At the bottom of the pub lies a secret whisky bar.

Copenhagen and Fuglen

In Copenhagen's Nrrebro district lies the café and cocktail bar Fuglen. The room is furnished with antique Nordic furniture and has a warm, nostalgic feel.

The cocktail menu offers both traditional and contemporary beverages, as well as a variety of sake and whiskies from Japan. During the day, Fuglen also offers coffee and small snacks.

Copenhagen's 10th Ved Stranden

A historic bar called Ved Stranden 10 may be found in the heart of Copenhagen. Since its founding in 1737, the pub has developed into a landmark in the community.

The room is furnished with antiques and has a warm, nostalgic feel about it. The bar provides a variety of traditional beverages, including aquavit, Danish beers, and old-fashioned gin and tonics.

Aalborg's The Barking Dog

In the heart of Aalborg, there is a craft beer pub called The Barking Dog. The bar serves a variety of wines, spirits, and a changing list of craft beers from across the world and Denmark. The area is furnished with old posters and has a relaxed, welcoming vibe.

Copenhagen to Brus

The brewery, pub, and restaurant Brus are situated in Copenhagen's Nrrebro district. Sour beers and barrel-aged beers are among the many types of beer that the brewery creates.

The pub serves a variety of Brus's speciality beers in addition to special guest taps from other Danish brewers. With a combination of concrete and wood materials, the room has an industrial and futuristic feel.

Aarhus to Lidkb

The cocktail bar Lidkb is situated in Aarhus' Latin Quarter. The pub has a warm and welcoming ambience and is set in a historic structure. Together with a variety of Danish spirits and beers, the cocktail menu offers both traditional and contemporary beverages. Moreover, a variety of small dishes and snacks are offered by Lidkb.

Copenhagen - Moosehead

Copenhagen's Vesterbro district is home to the craft beer pub Moosehead. The bar serves a variety of wines, spirits, and a changing list of craft beers from across the world and Denmark. The room has a warm, inviting ambience thanks to the antique design and furniture.

Copenhagen Taphouse

The Copenhagen city centre is home to the Taphouse, a craft beer pub. More than 60 Danish and foreign beers are available on tap in the bar, along with a wide variety of beers in bottles. With a mixture of concrete and metal, the room is contemporary and industrial.

Best Places to Shop

Copenhagen, Illum

High-end retailer Illum is situated in the centre of Copenhagen. Gucci, Prada, Chanel, and other high-end fashion, cosmetics, and lifestyle brands are among those sold at the shop. Together with several eateries and cafés, the market also has a gourmet food hall.

Copenhagen's Magasin du Nord

Another upscale department store in Copenhagen's city centre is Magasin du Nord. Burberry, Marc Jacobs, and Yves Saint Laurent are just a few of the many fashion, beauty, and lifestyle brands that are available at the shop. Together with several eateries and cafés, the market also has a gourmet food hall.

Copenhagen Hay House

Copenhagen's Vesterbro district is home to the design shop Hay House. The shop sells a variety of contemporary and minimalist home furnishings, lighting, and accessories. On the top level of Hay House, there is a café with a view of the city.

Copenhagen - Stilleben

Copenhagen's city centre is home to the design shop Stilleben. The shop has a variety of pottery, glassware, and home décor goods from Denmark and other countries. Moreover, Stilleben has a little café where coffee and light fare are served.

Copenhagen's Norse Store

In Copenhagen's Nrrebro district lies the fashion and leisure shop known as Norse Store. High-end clothes and accessories, as well as things for the home and beauty supplies, are all available at the shop. Moreover, Norse Store includes a café where coffee and light fare are served.

Copenhagen's Street

In the centre of Copenhagen, there is a pedestrian-only retail street called Street. A variety of high-end and mid-range fashion, beauty, and lifestyle retailers line the boulevard. There are several eateries and coffee shops on the Street.

Aarhus's Bruun's Galleri

In the heart of Aarhus, there is a retail mall called Bruun's Galleri. Zara, H&M, and Sephora are just a few of the many fashion, beauty, and lifestyle brands available in the centre. Bruun's Galleri also has several eateries and coffee shops.

Shop ARoS in Aarhus

Within the ARoS Aarhus Art Museum lies the ARoS Store, a museum shop. Together with a variety of Scandinavian clothing and home décor goods, the shop provides a collection of art books, prints, and design things. Moreover, ARoS Store features a café where coffee and light fare are served.

Copenhagen's Royal Denmark Flagship Store

In the heart of Copenhagen, you can find the Royal Copenhagen Flagship Shop. The shop sells a variety of hand-painted tableware, vases, and figures made of stoneware and porcelain. The shop also features a café where coffee and light fare are served.

Danish design firm Design Werck

A design shop called Design Werck is situated in Copenhagen's Vesterbro district. The shop has a variety of Danish and foreign furniture, lighting, and home furnishings. Moreover, Design Werck features a café where coffee and light fare are served.

Best Places to Stay

Denmark's Hotel d'Angleterre

In the centre of Copenhagen stands the five-star luxury hotel Hotel d'Angleterre. The hotel has tastefully furnished guestrooms and suites, a Michelin-starred dining room, and a rooftop terrace with expansive city views.

Hotel Nimb in Copenhagen

A five-star boutique hotel called Nimb Hotel is situated in Copenhagen's Tivoli Gardens. The hotel features opulent guestrooms and suites as well as several eating establishments, including a brasserie and a restaurant with a Michelin star.

Nielsen - Sanders

A five-star luxury hotel called Sanders may be found in Copenhagen's old town. Beautifully decorated guestrooms and suites, a restaurant featuring Danish food, and a welcoming bar with a fireplace are all available at the hotel.

Skt. Hotel. Copenhagen - Petri

Skt. Hotel. A five-star hotel called Petri is situated in Copenhagen's hip Latin District. A rooftop patio with city views, a restaurant offering Mediterranean food, and roomy bedrooms are all available at the hotel.

Skodsborg's Kurhotel Skodsborg

A five-star spa hotel called Kurhotel Skodsborg is situated not far from

Copenhagen. The hotel has opulent rooms and suites, a spa with a variety of treatments, and several eating establishments, including a Michelin-starred restaurant.

Copenhagen's Kokkedal Castle - Hrsholm

An ancient castle just north of Copenhagen is home to the five-star luxury hotel Kokkedal Castle Copenhagen. The hotel has a spa, and many eating choices, including a Michelin-starred restaurant, as well as tastefully furnished rooms and suites.

Aarhus Hotel Sanders

In the centre of Aarhus, there is a luxurious boutique hotel called Hotel Sanders. The hotel has elegantly designed guestrooms and suites, a rooftop patio with city views, and a Scandinavian restaurant.

Apartment in Copenhagen

A historic building in the centre of Copenhagen houses the five-star luxury hotel Villa Copenhagen. Beautifully furnished guestrooms and suites are available, along with a variety of eating establishments, including a rooftop bar and a restaurant providing sustainable cuisine.

Frederiksminde Hotel - Priest

A five-star hotel called Hotel Frederiksminde is situated on Zealand's shore, approximately an hour's drive from Copenhagen. Beautifully furnished rooms and suites, a restaurant featuring seasonal Nordic cuisine, and a spa are all features of the hotel.

Aslik Hotel in Snderborg

In the southern Danish town of Snderborg, near the coastline, sits the five-star Hotel Alsik. The hotel has opulent guestrooms and suites, a spa, and several eating establishments, including a rooftop bar with sweeping harbour views.

Aalborg's Hotel D'Angleterre

In the centre of Aalborg, there is a four-star luxury hotel called Hotel D'Angleterre. The hotel has tastefully decorated guestrooms and suites, a French-inspired restaurant, and a bar with a large range of wines and spirits.

The Royal Hotel in Aarhus

In the centre of Aarhus, there is a four-star boutique hotel called Hotel Royal. The hotel provides inviting, chic guestrooms and suites, a dining area with seasonal Scandinavian fare, and a welcoming bar.

Middelfart Comwell Kongebrogaarden

A four-star hotel called Comwell Kongebrogaarden is situated in Middelfart along the Little Belt. The hotel has contemporary, roomy rooms and suites, a restaurant providing foreign and Danish cuisine, and a spa with several different treatments.

Roskilde, Comwell, and Roskilde

A four-star hotel called Comwell Roskilde is situated not far from Roskilde's historic centre. The hotel has cosy guestrooms and suites, a restaurant offering seasonal Scandinavian cuisine, and a lounge bar.

Aarhus, Hotel Oasia Aarhus

In the centre of Aarhus, there is a four-star hotel called Hotel Oasia. The hotel has chic and contemporary guest rooms and suites, an international restaurant, and a rooftop patio with city views.

Comwell Rebild Bakker - Skripping

In the picturesque Rebild Hills next to Skrping, there is a four-star hotel called Comwell Rebild Bakker. The hotel has cosy guestrooms and suites, a dining establishment offering Scandinavian food, and a spa with a sauna, hot tub, and indoor pool.

Odense's First Hotel Grand

The Hans Christian Andersen birthplace of Odense is home to the four-star First Hotel Grand. The hotel has elegantly furnished guestrooms and suites, a dining area featuring Scandinavian cuisine, and a welcoming bar.

Spark Hotel - Maribo

On the island of Lolland, next to Maribo Lake, sits the three-star Hotel Spark. The hotel has cosy guestrooms and suites, a dining area with Danish food, and a patio with lake views.

Ballerup Hotel Lautrup Park

Located in the Ballerup neighbourhood in the suburb of Copenhagen, Hotel Lautrup Park is a three-star hotel. The hotel has cosy guestrooms and suites, an international restaurant, and a fitness facility.

Danish Hotel in Copenhagen

In Copenhagen's historic district sits the three-star Hotel Danmark. The hotel has cosy guestrooms and suites, a dining area offering both Danish and foreign fare, and a rooftop terrace with city views.

Possible itinerary for a 7-day and 10 days trips to Denmark

Denmark is a charming, little nation with a fascinating history and culture. It is home to a variety of intriguing cities, charming villages, and breathtaking natural landscapes that draw tourists from across the globe. A suggested schedule for a 7-day visit to Denmark is shown below:

First day: Copenhagen

Arriving in Copenhagen, the Danish capital. See the city's well-known attractions all day long, including the Little Mermaid monument, the vibrant Nyhavn port, and Tivoli Gardens. See the city from a new angle via canal boat, and then dine on some authentic Danish food at a nearby restaurant.

Copenhagen on Day 2

See several of Copenhagen's top-notch museums on another day, including the National Museum of Denmark and the Ny Carlsberg Glyptotek.

National Museum

Discover the hip Vesterbro and Nrrebro areas, which are filled with shops, cafés, and street art.

Vesterbro

3rd day: Aarhus

Drive or take a train to Aarhus, the
second-largest city in Denmark. To
observe how Danes formerly lived, go
visit the ARoS Aarhus Art Museum,
which is renowned for its

rainbow-coloured rooftop installation, and take a walk around the Old Town open-air museum. The Latin Quarter, which is teeming with bars and eateries, is a great place to spend a night out.

4th day: Aarhus

See some of Aarhus' lesser-known sites, such as the Marselisborg Deer Park and the Moesgaard Museum, which present the history and culture of Viking-era Denmark. Spend another day there.

5th day: Odense

Visit Odense, where renowned children's author Hans Christian Andersen was born. See the charming old town while learning about Hans

Christian Andersen's life and work at the Hans Christian Andersen Museum. One of the biggest and most well-known zoos in Denmark is the Odense Zoo, so be sure to visit it.

6th day: Roskilde

Visit the ancient city of Roskilde, once the capital of Denmark. Explore the Viking Ship Museum, which is home to five genuine Viking ships, and the UNESCO-listed Roskilde Cathedral, which serves as the last resting place for several Danish kings and queens.

Frederiksborg Castle on Day 7

Visit Frederiksborg Castle, one of the most magnificent Renaissance castles in Denmark. It is situated in Hilliard, just north of Copenhagen, and is surrounded by lovely gardens. It also houses a sizable collection of artwork, including sculptures and paintings.

This is just a suggested itinerary; you may easily alter it to fit your needs and timetable. Although Denmark is a tiny nation, travelling by automobile or public transportation is simple. To minimise disappointment, be sure to reserve lodging and activities in advance.

A detailed schedule for a 10-day visit to Denmark is provided below:

1st and 2nd day in Copenhagen

Explore Copenhagen's well-known sites, including the Round Tower, Christiansborg Palace, and the Botanical Gardens, over two full days.

Visit Torvehallerne food market and take a bike tour to see the city like a native while sampling the cuisine of Denmark.

3rd day: Ribe

Ribe Denmark Cathedral

Visit Ribe, the oldest settlement in Denmark, which has a wealth of historical structures and quaint alleys. To find out more about the town's unique past, visit the Ribe Cathedral and the Ribe Viking Museum.

Ribe Viking Museum

Esbjerg and the Wadden Sea on Day 4

Visit the Fisheries and Maritime Museum in Esbjerg for the day to learn about Danish fishing history. Next go to the Wadden Sea National Park, which is home to a distinctive ecosystem of mudflats, salt marshes, and dunes and is a UNESCO World Heritage Site.

5th day: Legoland

Visit Legoland in Billund, one of Denmark's finest family destinations. Discover the various rides, performances, and exhibitions at the park that are all built completely of Lego blocks.

6th day: Aarhus

Spend two additional days in Aarhus and take in the vibrant cultural scene. Visit the Aarhus Art Museum, the neighbouring Dokk1 library, and the cultural centre, and sample some of the delicious cuisine and beverages the city has to offer.

Mols Bjerge National Park on Day 7

Visit Mols Bjerge National Park, a
breathtaking region of hills, woods, and
beaches, on a day excursion. Explore
the stunning scenery by hiking, biking,
or riding a horse.

8th day: Odense

Upon your return, spend another day seeing Odense's many museums and tourist sites. Visit the Brandts Art Museum and Funen Village, an outdoor museum that depicts rural Danish life in the 19th century.

9th day: Roskilde

See the Viking Ship Museum and the neighbouring Roskilde Church when you return to Roskilde. Enjoy a fjord boat excursion to take in the breathtaking landscape.

Kronborg Castle on Day 10

Tour Kronborg Castle, a UNESCO World Heritage Site and the location for Shakespeare's "Hamlet." Enjoy the views of the Refund Strait while exploring the castle's many chambers and turrets.

This expanded schedule gives you the option to see additional locations and activities while also getting a better sense of Denmark's interesting culture and breathtaking scenery. Denmark is a great vacation spot for those who like history, culture, and outdoor activities since there is so much to see and do there.

Touring North Jutland: Home to Beautiful Scenery and Beaches

Beautiful North Jutland in Denmark offers breathtaking scenery, white sand beaches, and deep cultural history. These are some of the major attractions to take into account if you're considering visiting this region:

Lighthouse at Rubjerg Knude:

Built-in 1900, this lighthouse is situated atop a dune that has been steadily advancing inland for many years. Many of the nearby houses have recently been absorbed by the sand, leaving the lighthouse as a lone presence in the landscape.

Visitors may climb to the top of the lighthouse for breathtaking views of the surroundings, and they can also visit the adjoining museum to learn more about the history of the lighthouse.

Skagen:

In the northernmost point of Denmark, where the North Sea and the Baltic Sea converge, lies the town of Skagen. The town's stunning beaches, dunes, and distinctive light have long served as an inspiration to artists. These artists, notably the renowned Skagen painters, who portrayed the town's scenery and inhabitants in their paintings, have a collection of pieces on display in the Skagen Museum.

The Rbjerg Mile:

The biggest migratory dune in Northern Europe may be found here. A distinctive and ever-changing habitat is produced by the dune's ongoing movement, which also causes the surrounding terrain to change.

Visitors may join a guided tour to learn more about the dune's ecology and history, or they can climb to the summit of the dune for panoramic views of the surrounding area.

Aalborg:

The main city in North Jutland and the location of several historic buildings and cultural landmarks is Aalborg. A museum is presently housed in the 14th-century castle Aalborghus Castle, which lies in the heart of the city.

A merchant's home from the 16th century named Jens Bangs Stenhus has been conserved as a historical site. The Aalborg Zoo, the Kunsten Museum of Modern Art, and the Utzon Center, which exhibits the works of Danish architect Jrn Utzon, are further attractions.

Løkken:

The lovely coastal community of Løkken is well-known for its extensive sandy beaches and old-fashioned seaside appeal. Together with a historic lighthouse that may be climbed for sweeping views of the region, the town offers a bustling promenade packed with stores, eateries, and cafés.

Apart from relaxing on the beach and soaking up the sun, visitors may also try their hand at water sports like surfing.

Thy National Park

Dunes, heathlands, and marshes are all part of the enormous region of unspoiled natural splendour known as Thy National Park. The park's many paths allow for hiking and biking and also provide opportunities to see a variety of species, including deer, otters, and seals.

The Stenbjerg Landingsplads, which was used by Nazi forces during World War Two, is one of the park's many historic locations.

Aquarium at Hirtshals:

Many marine species, including sharks, rays, and sea turtles, may be found in this aquarium. By exploring underwater tunnels or taking in feeding displays, visitors may get up and personal with aquatic animals. Visitors to the aquarium may learn about the value of ocean conservation and the dangers that marine life faces in the aquarium's interactive displays.

Grenen:

Green, where the North Sea and the Baltic Sea converge, is where Denmark's northernmost point is located. To get to the spot where they may stand with one foot in each sea, visitors can stroll down the beach. A natural reserve in the region is also home to several bird species.

Sommerland, Frup:

North Jutland is home to the well-known amusement park Frup Sommerland. Around 60 rides and attractions, including water slides, roller coasters, and several family-friendly pursuits, can be found in the park. Families with kids will love Frup Sommerland since it has activities for guests of all ages.

Aarhus:

While Aarhus is technically not in North Jutland, it is close by and is the second-largest city in Denmark. The Aarhus Cathedral and the ARoS Aarhus Art Museum are only two examples of the city's blend of old and new buildings. The Aarhus Botanical Gardens, the Den Gamle By open-air museum, and the Moesgaard Museum are a few other attractions in Aarhus.

Blokhus:

Just south of Lkken lies the well-known coastal community of Blokhus. The community is renowned for its expansive, sandy beach, which is perfect for surfing, swimming, and sunbathing. Tourists may also meander through the quaint main street of the town, which is dotted with stores, eateries, and cafés.

Fjerritslev:

The centre of North Jutland is home to the little town of Fjerritslev. The town's mediaeval church, which was built in the 12th century, as well as its picturesque town square and modest stores and cafés, are among its most notable features.

The surrounding nature reserve, which is home to a variety of species and provides fantastic hiking and cycling options, is another place visitors may explore.

Bulbjerg:

The distinctive cliff structure known as Bulbjerg is situated on North Jutland's west coast. The cliffs, which climb up to 47 metres above the water, provide breathtaking views of the nearby shoreline. A natural reserve in the region is also home to several bird species.

Hirtshals:

North Jutland's western shore is home to the tiny fishing community of Hirtshals. The town is well-known for its bustling waterfront, which is home to several ferries and fishing vessels. Tourists may explore the adjacent beaches and dunes, wander along the port, or go to the aquarium in the area.

Jammerbugt:

In the northern region of North Jutland, there is a municipality called Jammerbugt. Forests, lakes, and beaches are among the area's stunning landscape features. Tourists may explore the area's many hiking and biking paths or cool down in one of the many lakes and swimming holes.

The Lnstrup Cliff, Vilsted Lake, and the Fosdalen Nature Reserve are a few of the further sights in Jammerbugt.

Conclusion

Beautiful North Jutland in Denmark offers a range of things for tourists to enjoy. Everyone may find something to enjoy in this scenic area, which offers everything from quaint coastal villages and gorgeous beaches to historic sites and nature reserves. North Jutland provides everything you might want, whether you're seeking outdoor recreation, cultural adventures, or just a peaceful vacation.

So, get your luggage and go to this stunning area for a trip you won't soon forget.

Experiencing Denmark's Culture: Food, Music, and Art

The culture of Denmark is extensive and varied, including art, music, and cuisine.

Here are some suggestions about how to fully appreciate each of these aspects of Danish culture:

Food

Danish cooking is distinguished by its concentration on straightforward, all-natural ingredients and local, seasonal products. Smrrebrd (open-faced sandwiches), frikadeller (meatballs), and aebleskiver are other popular Danish foods (pancake balls). Visit regional markets like

Torvehallerne in Copenhagen or the Aarhus Central Food Market in Aarhus to sample the finest of Danish cuisine. You may also dine at conventional Danish establishments like Copenhagen's Noma, which is renowned for its avant-garde, Nordic-inspired food.

Music

There are many different genres and kinds of music to discover in the booming Danish music industry. Agnes Obel, M, and Lukas Graham are a few of the most well-known Danish musicians.

Attend one of the numerous music festivals held throughout the year, including the Roskilde Festival or NorthSide Festival, to get a personal taste of Danish music. You may also go to music venues where both national and international acts perform, such as Vega in Copenhagen or Train in Aarhus.

Vega in Copenhagen

Danish art and design

Have a long history, and they are known for their emphasis on minimalist and practical aesthetics. The painter Vilhelm Hammershi and the designer Arne Jacobsen are two of the most well-known Danes.

Visit places like the ARoS Aarhus Art Museum in Aarhus or the National Gallery of Denmark in Copenhagen to explore Danish art. You may also browse the various design boutiques and galleries, like Copenhagen's Designmuseum Danmark, that feature the creations of regional artists and designers.

ARoS Aarhus Art Museum in Aarhus

*Copenhagen's Designmuseum
Danmark*

Any tourist seeking novel and interesting gastronomic experiences will be delighted by Denmark's rich and diversified culinary culture.

Some of the attractions of Danish gastronomy that make it a must-visit location for foodies include the following:

Danish open-faced sandwiches known as **shorebirds** are normally constructed with rye bread and topped with a variety of ingredients such as pickled herring, smoked salmon, or roast beef.

The outcome is a delightful and filling meal that is ideal for lunch or a light supper. The toppings are often coupled with creamy spreads like butter or mayonnaise.

Danish food, sometimes referred to as **"New Nordic Cuisine**," is renowned for being inventive and adventurous. This method of cooking places a strong emphasis on the utilisation of local, fresh foods as well as on simplicity and unprocessed tastes. This sort of food is a speciality of several of Denmark's best restaurants, including Noma in Copenhagen, which provides a unique and remarkable eating experience.

Danish pastries are a mainstay of Danish breakfasts and afternoon teas and are renowned for being sweet and flaky. The custard-filled "Berliner," the cinnamon bun (also known as a "kanelsnegl"), and the buttery "croissant" are some of the most well-known Danish pastries. For anybody with a sweet craving, these pastries are a must-try and are offered by bakeries all around the nation.

Seafood: Since Denmark is a nation bordered by water, seafood plays a significant role in the Danish diet. Fresh fish, such as salmon, cod, and herring, is often served across the nation on menus and is frequently cooked in a traditional Scandinavian manner, like smoking or pickling. Visit one of the numerous beach towns and fishing villages scattered around the coast for a real seafood experience.

Craft Beer: The craft beer industry is growing in Denmark, where several small brewers create distinctive, tasty beers that pay homage to regional ingredients and brewing customs. Mikkeller, Evil Twin, and To'l are among the most well-known Danish brews, and beer lovers may take part in a variety of festivals and sampling events all year long.

Generally speaking, Denmark has a rich and varied culinary culture that is likely to please any visitor. There is something for everyone to enjoy at this foodie's paradise, from classic open-faced sandwiches to creative New Nordic cuisine.

Traditional Danish meatballs known as **frikadeller** are created with a combination of ground beef and pig, onions, and breadcrumbs. They are a common comfort meal in Denmark and are often served with potatoes and a creamy sauce.

Rugbrd: A mainstay of the Danish diet, regard is a substantial and rich rye bread. It often serves as the foundation for shorebirds and tastes great when toasted with butter and cheese.

Flaeskesteg: Flaeskesteg is a traditional Danish meal prepared with crispy-skinned roast pork that is soft on the interior. Regular accompaniments include potatoes, red cabbage, and hearty gravy.

Little, round pancakes known as **"bleskiver"** are often consumed during the Christmas season. They are a tasty and festive dessert that is often packed with apple slices and coated with powdered sugar.

Gammel Dansk is a traditional herbal liqueur from Denmark that is often used as a digestif after dinner. It has a strong and unique taste that is both bitter and sweet and is created from a mix of 29 different herbs and spices.

Overall, Denmark has a vast selection of mouthwatering and distinctive cuisine that is likely to please any palette.

There is plenty to learn about and enjoy in this gastronomic wonderland of a nation, whether you like the inventive New Nordic food or the classic Nordic cuisine.

Understanding the Danish Way of Life: Customs and Traditions

Denmark is a country that prides itself on its rich cultural heritage, unique customs, and traditions. As a traveller to Denmark, it's important to understand the Danish way of life so that you can fully appreciate and respect their customs and traditions.

Here are some key things to keep in mind:

Hygge: One of the most famous Danish customs is "hygge," which roughly translates to cosiness or a sense of warmth and contentment. Danes love to create a cosy atmosphere, with candles, soft lighting, warm blankets, and good company. Embracing the concept of hygge is a great way to experience Danish culture.

Biking: Denmark is known for its bike-friendly culture, and you'll see plenty of Danes commuting to work or running errands on their bikes. Consider renting a bike to explore the city or countryside, but be sure to follow the rules of the road and bike paths.

Food: Denmark is famous for its cuisine, including open-faced sandwiches, pickled herring, and the ubiquitous Danish pastry. Be sure to try these traditional dishes, and don't be afraid to sample some of the more unusual ingredients, like liquorice or seaweed.

Respect personal space: Danes value their personal space and privacy, so it's important to be respectful of this. Avoid standing too close or touching strangers, and keep your voice down in public places.

Tipping: Tipping is not expected in Denmark, as service charges are usually included in the bill. However, it is still customary to round up the bill or leave a small tip for exceptional service.

Social equality: Danes pride themselves on their commitment to social equality, and you'll notice this in many aspects of daily life. For example, it's common to see CEOs riding bikes to work or politicians taking public transportation.

Jante Law: The Jante Law is a concept in Danish culture that emphasizes modesty, equality, and not standing out from the crowd. While it's not necessarily a law, it's deeply ingrained in Danish culture and something to be aware of as a traveller.

Sustainability: Denmark is a leader in sustainable living, and you'll notice this in many aspects of daily life, from the abundance of bike paths to the focus on renewable energy. Be sure to do your part as a responsible traveller by reducing your environmental impact.

By keeping these customs and traditions in mind, you'll be well on your way to understanding the Danish way of life and enjoying your time in this beautiful country.

Punctuality: Danes are generally very punctual, so it's important to be on time for meetings and appointments. Being late can be seen as disrespectful or rude, so make sure to plan and arrive on time.

Dress Code: Denmark has a casual dress code, but it's still important to dress appropriately for the occasion. Avoid wearing overly revealing or flashy clothing, especially in more formal settings.

Christmas traditions: Christmas is a big celebration in Denmark, with many unique traditions. One of the most well-known is the lighting of the

Christmas tree on December 23rd, followed by a festive dinner with family and friends on Christmas Eve.

Respect for nature: Denmark has a deep respect for nature, and you'll notice this in the way they care for their environment. It's important to be respectful of this and avoid littering or damaging natural areas.

Personal responsibility: Danes value personal responsibility, and it's important to take ownership of your actions and their consequences. If you make a mistake or cause harm, apologize and take steps to make things right.

Small talk: Danes are generally reserved and may not engage in small talk with strangers or acquaintances. However, once you get to know them, they can be very friendly and welcoming.

Flag flying: Denmark is proud of its flag, and you'll see it flying on many public buildings and homes. Be respectful of this national symbol and avoid any behaviour that may be seen as disrespectful.

Overall, Denmark is a wonderful country to visit, with a rich culture and many unique customs and traditions. By being respectful and open-minded, you'll have a fantastic experience and

gain a deeper understanding of Danish
life.

Outdoor Activities in Denmark That you can participate on: Hiking, Biking, and More

Denmark offers a wide range of outdoor activities for travellers to participate in.

Here are some popular ones:

Hiking:

Several hiking paths in Denmark go through stunning woods, national parks, and coastal regions. A short 30-minute drive from Copenhagen is the Grib Forest, the Mols Bjerge National Park on Jutland's east coast, and the Jutland Ridge, which traverses the western portion of the island. In Denmark, hiking is a fantastic opportunity to see the country's scenic splendour and burn some calories at the same time.

Biking:

Due to its extensive network of bike lanes and riding routes, Denmark is regarded as one of the world's cycle-friendliest nations. To explore the city or the countryside, cyclists may hire a bike or join a guided trip.

The Baltic Sea Route, which follows Jutland's eastern coast, and the North Sea Route, which follows Jutland's western coast, are two of the most well-known cycling routes. A fun and environmentally responsible method to get to Denmark is by bicycle.

Canoeing and kayaking:

Kayaking and canoeing are ideal in Denmark's abundant lakes, rivers, and coastal locations. Sea kayaking is popular in the South Funen Archipelago, and canoeing may be done in the calm waters of the Limfjord. Kayaking is a popular activity on Denmark's longest river, the Guden River. In Denmark, kayaking and canoeing are wonderful ways to appreciate the country's rivers and get close to nature.

Surfing:

Denmark offers numerous top-notch surfing locations, particularly along Jutland's west coast. One of the top surfing sites in Denmark is Klitmller, sometimes known as Cold Hawaii, and it attracts surfers from all over the globe. Another well-liked location for windsurfing is Hvide Sande. A fantastic way to take in Denmark's coastline is to surf.

Beach Recreation

Beautiful beaches in Denmark are great for swimming, tanning, and beach volleyball. One of Denmark's most well-known beaches is Skagen Beach, which is situated on Jutland's most northern point. The north shore of Zealand's Tisvildeleje Beach is a well-liked location for swimming and tanning.

One of the longest beaches in Denmark, Marielyst Beach is situated on Zealand's south coast and is a well-liked destination for beach activities. In Denmark, beach activities are a wonderful opportunity to unwind and take in the sunshine and sand.

wildlife observation

Seals, birds, and deer are among the many species of animals that call Denmark's various nature reserves and parks home. In southwest Jutland, the Wadden Sea National Park is a UNESCO World Heritage Site and is home to several bird species, especially migratory birds.

The east coast of Jutland's Mols Bjerge National Park is home to a wide variety of species, including deer and wild boar.

In Denmark, wildlife viewing is a wonderful opportunity to come in touch with nature and discover the local fauna.

Camping:

An excellent place to go camping is Denmark, which has a lot of campgrounds spread out over the nation. On Jutland's most northern point, Skagen Campsite and Feriecenter is a well-liked campground with beach access.

Kvie S Campsite is a kid-friendly campground with a playground and activities like mini-golf in western Jutland.

Southern Jutland's Ribe Campsite is a well-liked campground with proximity to the Wadden Sea National Park. Denmark's natural beauty and the great outdoors may both be experienced when camping.

Climbing rocks:

Rock climbing is quite popular in Denmark, notably in the Mns Klint region on the island of Mn. A UNESCO World Heritage Site, Mns Klint is well known for its imposing white chalk cliffs.

For those eager to attempt rock climbing for the first time, the cliffs provide both a difficult ascent and a unique experience. A fantastic way to enjoy Denmark's breathtaking scenery is to go rock climbing.

Equine Riding:

Several horseback riding paths in Denmark go through stunning farms, woods, and coastal regions. Horseback riding trips that take you over the dunes and down the coastline are available at the Skagen Odde Nature Centre, which is situated in the northernmost part of Jutland.

Moreover, horseback riding excursions through the marshes and along the shore are available in the Danish Wadden Sea National Park. In Denmark, riding a horse is a wonderful opportunity to both enjoy the country's natural beauty and get some exercise.

Golfing:

Numerous top-notch golf courses in Denmark provide difficult play and breathtaking scenery. One of the top golf courses in Europe is the Scandinavian Golf Club, which is situated in the northern part of Copenhagen. The centrally situated Silkeborg Ry Golf Club has an 18-hole course that is difficult and is set in lovely surroundings. Jutland. Two holes at the R Golf Club in northern Jutland provide breathtaking views of the North Sea.

Fishing:

Denmark is an excellent place to go fishing since there are so many lakes, rivers, and coastal regions where you may do it. Salmon, trout, and pike are among the species that may be caught in the Guden River, making it a well-liked location for fishing. Cod, mackerel, and places are among the species that may be caught while sea fishing in Jutland's coastal regions.

Sailing:

Denmark's extensive coastline and plenty of marinas provide chances for sailing for both novice and expert sailors. With its tranquil waters and picturesque surroundings, the Limfjord is a well-liked sailing location. With its abundance of islands and charming harbours, the Danish South Sea is another well-liked location for sailing. A wonderful way to appreciate Denmark's beautiful coastline and take in the sea air is to go sailing.

Kiteboarding:

Denmark is a fantastic place to do kiteboarding since several locations along the shore provide ideal weather for the activity. Denmark's Ringkbing Fjord, with its flat water and high winds, is one of the greatest places for kiteboarding.

Along with waves and powerful gusts, Klitmller is a well-liked location for kiteboarding. In Denmark, kiteboarding is an exhilarating way to enjoy the coastline and get your heart beating.

Viewing birds:

Birds of many different kinds may be found across Denmark, although they are most numerous along the shore and in nature reserves. A well-liked location for bird viewing is the Wadden Sea National Park, where migrating birds often pass through.

Several different bird species may be seen in the Skagen Odde Nature Centre, which is a well-known location for birdwatching. These birds can be seen on the dunes and along the shore. In Denmark, bird watching is a wonderful opportunity to go outside and discover the biodiversity of the nation.

Skiing:

Although Denmark may not be the first destination that springs to mind when considering skiing, there are several ski resorts there that provide both skiing and snowboarding.

A few miles outside of Copenhagen, the Hareskovby Ski Complex has various ski lines and artificial snow. A terrain park and several ski lines are available at the Silkeborg Ski Centre in the heart of Jutland.

Conclusion

For tourists who adore the great outdoors, Denmark provides a variety of outdoor activities. There is something for everyone, from bicycling and hiking to rock climbing and equestrian riding. The gorgeous scenery, coastline, and natural reserves of the nation provide the ideal setting for these activities.

Denmark also features a lot of golf courses, fishing holes, sailing ports, kiteboarding locations, bird viewing locations, and even ski resorts. These pursuits not only provide a wonderful opportunity to take in the natural beauty of the nation but also present a chance to get some exercise and your heart rate up.

Those who wish to experience the great outdoors and take in the breathtaking landscape may consider visiting Denmark.

Exploring Danish History: Castles, Museums, and Landmarks

15 castles, museums, and landmarks to explore in Denmark:

1. Kronborg Castle:

Kronborg Castle is a beautiful Renaissance castle located in the town of Helsingør, about 45 minutes north of Copenhagen. It was built in the 16th century and has played an important role in Danish history, serving as a fortress and a royal palace.

The castle is best known as the setting for Shakespeare's play "Hamlet," and visitors can explore the various rooms and halls of the castle, including the grand ballroom and the chapel. The castle is also home to several museums, including the Royal Danish Maritime Museum and the Danish National Maritime Museum.

2. Frederiksborg Castle:

Located in Hillerød, about 30 minutes north of Copenhagen, Frederiksborg Castle is a magnificent Renaissance palace built in the early 17th century. The castle was built by King Christian IV and served as the royal residence until the 19th century.

Today, the castle houses the Museum of National History, which features a collection of paintings, sculptures, and artefacts that tell the story of Danish history from the Middle Ages to the present day. Visitors can also explore

the castle's beautiful gardens and
grounds.

3. The Viking Ship Museum:

The Viking Ship Museum is located in
Roskilde, about 30 minutes west of
Copenhagen. The museum is dedicated
to the history and culture of the Vikings
and features a collection of five Viking
ships that were excavated from the
nearby fjord.

Visitors can learn about the Viking Age
and see the ships up close, as well as
participate in various hands-on
activities, such as building a model
Viking ship or trying on Viking clothes.
The museum also offers sailing trips on
a reconstructed Viking ship.

4. The National Museum of Denmark:

The National Museum of Denmark is located in Copenhagen and is the largest museum of cultural history in the country. The museum features exhibits on Danish prehistory, the Middle Ages, and modern history, as well as collections of coins, medals, and ethnographic objects.

Highlights of the museum include the Viking Age exhibit, which features a collection of Viartefactsfacts and displays, and the Royal Danish Antiquities collection, which showcases Denmark's cultural heritage.

5. Tivoli Gardens:

Tivoli Gardens is a historic amusement park located in the heart of Copenhagen. The park was founded in 1843 and is one of the oldest amusement parks in the world. Visitors can enjoy a variety of rides and attractions, including roller coasters, carnival games, and live entertainment.

The park also features beautiful gardens, fountains, and architecture, and is a popular destination for tourists and locals alike.

6. The Little Mermaid:

The Little Mermaid is a bronze statue located in Copenhharbour Harbor. The statue was inspired by the Hans Christian Andersen fairy tale of the same name and was created by sculptor Edvard Eriksen in 1913.

The statue has become a symbol of Copenhagen and is one of the city's most popular tourist attractions. Visitors can take a photo with the statue and enjoy the views harbour harbour.

7. The Round Tower:

The Round Tower is a historic tower locatedcentreecentrerinf Copenhagen. The tower was built in the 17th century and features a unique spiral ramp instead of stairs.

Visitors can climb to the top of the tower and enjoy panoramic views of the city. The tower also houses an observatory and a library.

8. Christiansborg Palace:

Christiansborg Palace is a palace complex located on the island of Slotsholmen in Copenhagen. The palace is home to the Danish Parliament, the Prime Minister's Office, and the Supreme Court of Denmark.

Visitors can take a guided tour of the palace and explore its various halls and rooms, including the throne room, the Great Hall, and the Royal Stables. The palace also houses several museums, including the Royal Reception Rooms, which feature exhibits on the monarchy and Danish history.

9. The Rosenborg Castle:

The Rosenborg Castle is a beautiful Renaissance castle located in the Copenhagcentreity centre. The castle was built in the 17th century as a summer residence for King Christian IV and is now open to the public as a museum.

Visitors can explore the castle's various rooms and halls, including the King's Bedroom, the Knight's Hall, and the Treasury, which houses the Danish Crown Jewels.

10. The National Gallery of Denmark:

The National Gallery of Denmark, also known as the SMK, is Denmark's largest art museum and is located in Copenhagen. The museum features a collection of Danish and international art from the 14th century to the present day, including works by famous artists such as Rembrandt, Picasso, and Matisse.

The museum also houses a collection of Danish Golden Age paintings, as well as a collection of contemporary art.

11. The Møns Klint:

Møns Klint is a stunning cliff formation located on the island of Møn in southeastern Denmark. The cliffs are made of ck and rise to 128 meters above the Baltic Sea.

Visitors can take a hike along the cliffs and enjoy the breathtaking views of the sea and the surrounding landscape. The area is also home to a variety of wildlife, including falcons and seals.

12. The Aarhus Cathedral:

The Aarhus Cathedral is a beautiful Gothic cathedral located in the city of Aarhus, in central Jutland. The cathedral was built in the 13th century and is one of Denmark's oldest and most impressive churches.

Visitors can explore the cathedral's various chapels, crypts, and altars, as well as admire its impressive stained glass windows and sculptures.

13. The Egeskov Castle:

The Egeskov Castle is a stunning Renaissance castle located on the island of Funen, in central Denmark. The castle was built in the 16th century and is surrounded by a moat and beautiful gardens.

Visitors can explore the castle's various rooms and halls, including the Knight's Hall, the Music Room, and the Dining Room. The castle also houses several museums, including a collection of vintage cars and motorcycles.

14. The Skagen Odde National Park:

The Skagen Odde National Park is a beautiful nature reserve located on the northern tip of Jutland Pand ark features dunes, heathlands, and beaches, as well as a variety of wildlife, including deer, seals, and sea birds.

Visitors can hike along the park's many trails and enjoy the stunning views of the sea and the surrounding landscape.

15. The Ribe Cathedral:

The Ribe Cathedral is a beautiful Romanesque cathedral located in the town of Ribe, in southwestern

Denmark. The cathedral was built in the 12th century and is one of Denmark's oldest churches.

Visitors can explore the cathedral's various chapels and altars, as well as admire its impressive frescoes and sculptures. The cathedral also houses a museum with exhibits on the history of the church and the town of Ribe.

Conclusion

Denmark has a rich history and culture, and there are many castles, museums, and landmarks that provide insight into the country's past and present. From the impressive Frederiksborg Castle and its beautiful gardens to the stunning Møns

Klint cliff formation and the charming town of Tivoli Gardens, there travelling for every traveller to explore.

Visitors can also learn about Danish art and history at museums such as the National Gallery of Denmark and the Royal Reception Rooms, or experience the natural beauty of Denmark's parks and nature reserves, such as the Skagen Odde National Park. Whether you're interested in history, art, or nature, Denmark offers a wealth of fascinating destinations to discover.

Accommodations in Denmark: Hotels, Hostels, and Vacation Rentals

Denmark offers a wide range of accommodations for travellers, including hotels, hostels, and vacation rentals. Here is an overview of each option:

Hotels

Hotels in Denmark range from budget-friendly options to luxury accommodations. Most hotels in Denmark offer amenities such as free Wi-Fi, breakfast, and housekeeping services.

Some hotels may also have on-site restaurants, fitness centres, or conference rooms. Denmark has many international hotel chains, including Radisson Blu, Scandic, and Marriott, as well as smaller independent hotels. Prices for hotels vary depending on the location, season, and level of luxury.

Hostels

Hostels in Denmark offer a budget-friendly option for travellers, particularly backpackers and solo travellers. Most hostels offer both shared and private rooms, and some may have dormitory-style rooms with bunk beds.

Hostels typically offer basic amenities such as free Wi-Fi, communal kitchen and lounge areas, and sometimes breakfast. Some hostels may also offer additional services such as bicycle rentals or tour booking.

Hostels in Denmark are generally located in urban areas and near popular tourist attractions. Popular hostel chains in Denmark include Danhostel and Hostelling International.

Vacation Rentals

Vacation rentals in Denmark are a popular option for travellers who want more space and privacy. These rentals include apartments, houses, and villas that are rented out to travellers for short-term stays.

Vacation rentals in Denmark can be found through websites such as Airbnb, Vrbo, and Booking.com. They offer many amenities such as a fully equipped kitchen, free Wi-Fi, and sometimes a washer and dryer. Some vacation rentals may also have outdoor spaces, such as patios or gardens. Prices for vacation rentals vary depending on the location, season, and level of luxury.

Overall, the type of accommodation you choose in Denmark will depend on your budget and travel preferences. Hotels offer a range of options from budget-friendly to luxury, hostels are a great option for budget-conscious travellers, and vacation rentals offer space and privacy for those looking for a more homely experience.

Here are some important factors to consider when choosing between

hotels, hostels, and vacation rentals in Denmark:

Hotels:

Location: Consider the location of the hotel the activities you plan to do and the transportation options available.

Price: Hotels in Denmark can vary greatly in price, so consider your budget and what amenities you need.

Amenities: Look for hotels that offer amenities that are important to you, such as free Wi-Fi, breakfast, and fitness facilities.

Room size and type: Consider how many people are travelling with you and what type of room you need, such as a single, double, or suite.

Brand reputation: Consider the reputation of the hotel brand and read reviews from previous guests to ensure a quality experience.

Hostels:

Location: Hostels are often located in urban areas and near popular tourist attractions, so consider the location of the activities you plan to do.

Price: Hostels offer a budget-friendly option, so consider the price and what amenities are included.

Room type: Hostels offer both shared and private rooms, so consider your preference and budget.

Amenities: Look for hostels that offer amenities that are important to you, such as free Wi-Fi, communal kitchen and lounge areas, and bicycle rentals.

Reputation: Consider the reputation of the hostel brand and read reviews from previous guests to ensure a quality experience.

Vacation Rentals:

Location: Vacation rentals are often located in residential areas, so consider the location of the activities you plan to do and the transportation options available.

Price: Vacation rentals can vary greatly in price, so consider your budget and what amenities you need.

Amenities: Look for vacation rentals that offer amenities that are important to you, such as a fully equipped kitchen, free Wi-Fi, and outdoor spaces.

Size: Consider the size of the rental and whether it can accommodate the number of people in your group.

Reputation: Read reviews from previous guests to ensure a quality experience and consider renting from a reputable website such as Airbnb or Vrbo.

Overall, when choosing between hotels, hostels, and vacation rentals in Denmark, consider your budget, travel preferences, and what amenities are important to you.

The type of accommodation you choose in Denmark will depend on your budget and travel preferences. Hotels offer a range of options from budget-friendly to luxury, hostels are a great option for budget-conscious travellers, and vacation rentals offer space and privacy for those looking for a more homely experience.

In conclusion, Denmark offers a range of accommodations for travellers, including hotels, hostels, and vacation rentals. Each type of accommodation has its unique features and benefits, and the choice ultimately depends on your budget, travel preferences, and the amenities you need.

Hotels offer a range of options from budget-friendly to luxury, hostels are a great option for budget-conscious travellers, and vacation rentals offer space and privacy for those looking for a more homely experience.

When choosing between these options, consider important factors such as location, price, amenities, room size and type, and reputation. By doing so, you can find the best accommodation option for your trip to Denmark.

Transportation in Denmark: Getting Around with Ease

Denmark has a well-developed transportation system that makes it easy to get around the country.

Here are some of the transportation options available to you in Denmark:

Public Transportation: Denmark has an extensive public transportation system consisting of buses, trains, and metros. The system is run by several operators, including DSB (Danish State Railways) and Movia (buses). Public transport is efficient, reliable, and covers most areas of the country.

Cycling: Denmark is a cycling-friendly country with well-marked cycle paths, and bicycles can be rented at many locations across the country. Many cities also have bike-sharing schemes that allow you to rent a bike for a short period.

Driving: If you prefer to drive, you can rent a car from one of the many car rental companies located in Denmark. It is essential to note that driving in Denmark can be expensive due to the high cost of petrol and tolls.

Taxis: Taxis are available in Denmark but can be quite expensive compared to public transport.

Ferries: Denmark has many islands, and ferries are the most convenient way to travel between them. You can book ferry tickets online or at the port.

Overall, public transportation and cycling are the most affordable and efficient ways to get around Denmark. The country's small size and well-connected transport system make it easy to explore all that Denmark has to offer.

Here's some more information on each transportation option in Denmark:

Public Transportation

1. Trains

Denmark's train system is operated by DSB, which is a state-owned company. Trains run frequently, and you can purchase tickets online or at vending machines located at the train stations.

There are several different types of trains, including regional trains, which connect smaller towns, and intercity trains, which travel between major cities. The intercity trains are the fastest and most comfortable, but they are also the most expensive.

Important points:

- Some trains require a seat reservation, so it's essential to check before boarding.

- There are discounts available for children, students, and seniors.

- Most trains have wifi and power outlets, so you can work or stay connected during your journey.

2. Buses

Movia operates most of the bus services in Denmark, and they run frequently and cover most areas of the country. Buses are an affordable way to travel between towns and cities, and you can purchase tickets online or at vending machines located at bus stops.

Important points:

- It's essential to check the timetable before travelling, as some buses may not run on weekends or holidays.

- Some buses have limited space for luggage, so it's important to pack light.

- You can save money by purchasing a travel card or a 10-trip ticket, which offers discounts on the regular fare.

3. Metro

Copenhagen's metro system is efficient, fast, and easy to use. It consists of two lines, which run from early morning until late at night. Tickets can be purchased at vending machines located at the stations, or through a mobile app.

Important points:

- The metro is the fastest way to get around Copenhagen, but it only serves a limited area of the city.

- You should keep your ticket until the end of your journey, as it may be checked by ticket inspectors.

- The metro is fully accessible for wheelchair users and people with disabilities.

4. Cycling

Denmark is known for being a cycling-friendly country, and many people use bicycles as their primary mode of transportation. You can rent a bike from several locations across the country, including in cities, towns, and tourist destinations. There are several types of bikes available for rent, including city bikes, electric bikes, and cargo bikes.

Important points:

- Denmark has a well-developed network of cycle paths, which makes cycling safe and enjoyable.

- You can plan your route using the Cycle Route Planner, which is an online tool that shows the best cycle routes in Denmark.

- Bikes are allowed on trains and buses, but there may be restrictions during peak hours.

5. Driving

Renting a car is an option in Denmark, but it is an expensive way to travel due to the high cost of petrol, tolls, and parking. Denmark drives on the right side of the road, and speed limits are in kilometres per hour.

Important points:

- It's important to have a valid driver's license and be at least 18 years old to rent a car in Denmark.

- Denmark has a toll system called BroBizz, which allows you to pay for tolls automatically.

- Parking can be difficult and expensive in cities, so it's best to use public transportation or cycle when possible.

6. Taxis

Taxis are available in Denmark, but they can be expensive compared to public transportation. Taxis can be flagged down on the street or booked through a taxi company or app. The fare is calculated based on the distatravelledeled and the time of day.

Important points:

- Tipping is not customary in Denmark, but rounding up to the nearest whole number is common.

- You should make sure the taxi meter is turned on when you start your journey to ensure that you are charged the correct fare.

- It's always a good idea to ask for an estimate of the fare before getting into the taxi.

7. Ferries

Denmark is made up of several islands, so ferries are an important transportation option for getting between several ferry companies operate rate in Denmark, including DFDS and Molslinjen. You can purchase tickets online or at the ferry terminal.

Important points:

- Some ferries require reservations, so it's important to check betravellingeling.

- The journey time can vary depending on the destination, but most ferries offer onboard amenities such as cafes and shops.

- If you plan to bring a car on the ferry, it's important to book in advance, as space can be limited.

Overall, Denmark has a well-developed and efficient transportation system that makes it easy to get around the country. Public transportation is affordable and covers most areas of the country, and cycling is a popular and safe option.

While driving and taxis are available, they can be expensive and may not be the most convenient option in cities. Ferries are also an important transportation option for getting between Denmark's many islands.

Practical Information for Travelers going to Denmark: Currency, Language, and Safety

Denmark is a beautiful Scandinavian country that attracts millions of visitors every year. Here is some practical information for travelers visiting Denmark:

Currency:

The currency used in Denmark is the Danish krone (DKK). It is advisable to carry some cash for small purchases, but most shops and restaurants accept credit cards.

ATMs are widely available throughout the country.

Important points:

1. It is advisable to exchange your currency to Danish krone in Denmark rather than in your home country as the exchange rate may be better.

2. When using ATMs, be aware of skimming devices and use only trusted ones in well-lit areas.

Language:

The official language of Denmark is Danish, but most Danes also speak fluent English.

Important points:

1. It is always polite to learn a few basic Danish phrases such as "Tak" (thank you) and "Undskyld" (excuse me) to show respect for the local culture.

2. If you need assistance, it is recommended to approach younger Danes as they are more likely to speak English.

Safety:
Denmark is considered a safe country to travel to with low crime rates. However,

it is always advisable to take basic safety precautions.

Important points:

1. Keep your valuables safe, especially in crowded tourist areas.

2. Be cautious when using public transportation at night, and always travel in well-lit areas.

3. When cycling, wear a helmet, and follow the traffic rules as bikes are a popular mode of transportation in Denmark.

In conclusion, Denmark is a welcoming and safe country to travel to with friendly people, a vibrant culture, and a rich history. By following these practical tips, you can have an enjoyable and stress-free trip.

Making the Most of Your Trip: Tips and Tricks for a Memorable Experience

Denmark is a beautiful country filled with rich history, stunning architecture, and a unique culture. Whether you're planning to visit for the first time or you're a seasoned traveler, here are some tips and tricks to make the most of your trip to Denmark and ensure a memorable experience:

Explore Copenhagen: Denmark's capital city is a must-visit destination. You can stroll through the historic Nyhavn harbor, visit the Little Mermaid statue, or marvel at the Tivoli Gardens amusement park.

Rent a bike: Denmark is known for its cycling culture, and renting a bike is a great way to explore the city and its surroundings. There are plenty of bike rental shops in Copenhagen and other major cities, and many hotels also offer bike rentals.

Try the local cuisine: Danish cuisine is hearty and flavorful, with dishes like smørrebrød (open-faced sandwiches), frikadeller (meatballs), and flæskesteg (roast pork). Make sure to try some of the local specialties while you're in Denmark.

Visit the castles: Denmark is home to many beautiful castles and palaces, including Frederiksborg Castle, Kronborg Castle (the setting of Shakespeare's Hamlet), and Amalienborg Palace, the home of the Danish royal family.

Learn about Viking history: Denmark has a rich Viking history, and there are many museums and historical sites where you can learn about this fascinating period in Danish history. The Viking Ship Museum in Roskilde is a must-visit for anyone interested in Viking history.

Take a day trip: Denmark is a small country, and it's easy to explore other parts of the country on a day trip. Consider visiting the charming town of Odense, the birthplace of Hans Christian Andersen, or the picturesque island of Ærø.

Embrace hygge: Hygge is a Danish concept that is all about coziness, relaxation, and enjoying life's simple pleasures. Take some time to embrace hygge while you're in Denmark by enjoying a cup of hot cocoa, lighting some candles, or curling up with a good book.

Use public transportation: Denmark has an excellent public transportation system, including trains, buses, and metro lines. Using public transportation is an easy and affordable way to get around the country.

Dress for the weather: Denmark's weather can be unpredictable, so make sure to pack layers and dress for the weather. It's always a good idea to bring a raincoat and waterproof shoes, as Denmark can be rainy at any time of year.

Be respectful of Danish culture:
Danes are known for their friendly and welcoming nature, but it's important to be respectful of their culture and customs. Learn a few basic Danish phrases, follow local etiquette, and be mindful of cultural differences to ensure a positive experience in Denmark.

Printed in Great Britain
by Amazon

22410436R00116